The Prodigal Son

Luke 15:11-32

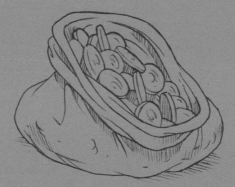

RETOLD BY MARY BERENDES • ILLUSTRATED BY ROBERT SQUIER

Distributed by The Child's World®
1980 Lookout Drive • Mankato, MN 56003-1705
800-599-READ • www.childsworld.com

ACKNOWLEDGMENTS
The Child's World®: Mary Berendes, Publishing Director
The Design Lab: Art Direction and Design
Red Line Editorial: Contributing Editor
Natalie Mortensen: Contributing Editor

LIBRARY OF CONGRESS CATALOGING-IN-PUBLICATION DATA
Berendes, Mary.
 The prodigal son / by Mary Berendes; illustrated by Robert Squier.
   p. cm.
 ISBN 978-1-60954-393-8 (library reinforced: alk. paper)
 1. Prodigal son (Parable)—Juvenile literature. I. Squier, Robert. II. Title.
 BT378.P8B35 2011
 226.8'09505—dc22   2011004958

Printed in the United States of America in Mankato, Minnesota.
July 2011
PA02087

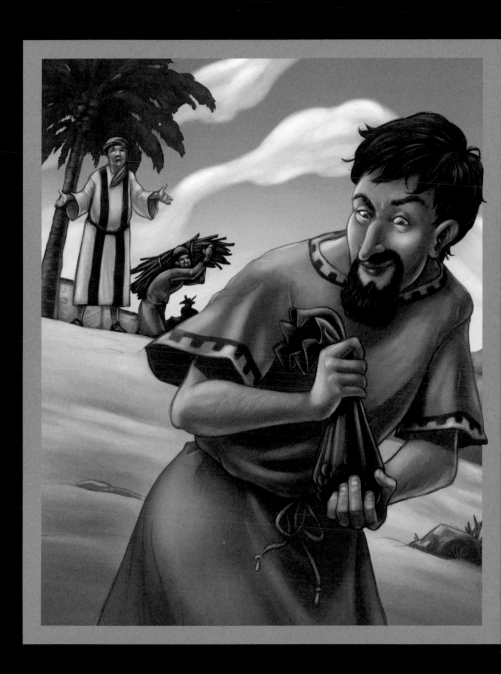

The parables of the Bible are simple, easy-to-remember stories that Jesus told. Even though the stories are simple, they have deeper meanings.

A crowd of people sat around Jesus one day. He told them a story:

———◆———

There once was a farmer who had two sons. The younger son said to his father, "Father, let me have my share of the money from our farm."

The father gave the younger son his money. The son left home and traveled far away. Over time, the son spent all of his money. He threw parties and ate and drank. He was careless and wasteful.

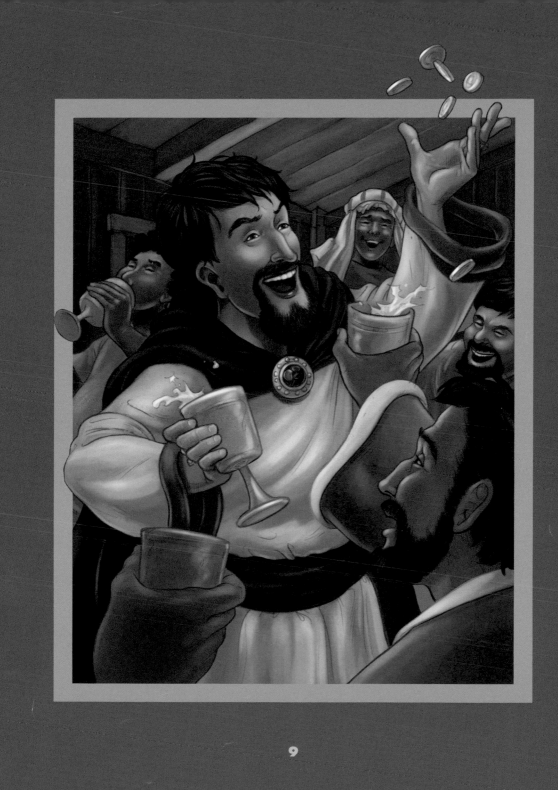

With his money all spent,
the son could not buy food.
He was hungry and cold. He
searched for work, but could
only find a job feeding pigs.
The son was so hungry, he
longed to eat the garbage the
pigs were eating.

The son was miserable.
He wanted to return home,
but he was afraid his father
would be angry. The son
thought and thought. Finally,
the son decided that he would
return home and beg his
father's forgiveness.

The son walked a long
time. When he neared his
family farm, his father saw
him coming. The father cried
and ran to his son. He kissed
him and hugged him tightly.

The son said, "Father, I have behaved terribly. I am not worthy to be called your son."

But the father said to the servants, "Bring fresh clothes for my son! Begin roasting some meat and playing music! We must celebrate. My son who had left us is back once more!"

When the older son came home, he saw the big party for his brother. He was angry and said to his father, "I have always been a good son. I have never disobeyed you or wasted your money. But you have never even thrown me a small party! Why?"

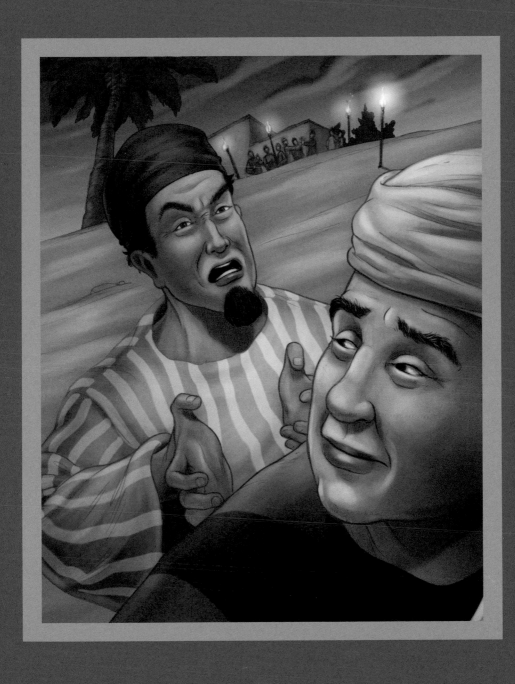

The father said to the oldest son, "You are always with me. We are able to eat together and talk every day. But we must celebrate for your brother. He was once lost, and is now found again!"

BEYOND THE STORY

Jesus uses the parable of the prodigal son to show us just how great God's love is for us. In the story the younger son is eager to go out into the world. He wants his inheritance from his father so he can afford to go. An inheritance is a share of what your family owns. Children often receive it after their parents die. The farmer freely gives his younger son the money. Instead of using the money wisely, the son wastes it all. The son's attitude and actions show he is selfish and immature.

The son sinks so low that he takes the only job he can get—feeding pigs. Pigs were considered unclean animals. During Jesus' time, Jews weren't even allowed to touch them. The son's taking a job tending pigs represents those people who are rebelling against God. Jesus helps us understand that sometimes you have to hit rock bottom before you can face your sins. Then you can start to fix your relationship with God. The son comes to his senses and returns to his father to beg for his forgiveness and mercy.

The father in the story welcomes his son back just like God welcomes sinners back. God is willing to forgive us after we come to him seeking forgiveness and compassion. God doesn't look back on our past sins. He simply celebrates that our relationship with him is right again and offers us everything in his kingdom.

The older brother represents the Pharisees. A Pharisee was a member of the Jewish faith who strictly observed all of their religious laws. The older brother is bitter and resentful of the attention the father shows to the younger son. He thinks since he has followed all of the rules, he should get all of his father's attention. What he doesn't realize is that he gets to share in his father's treasure every day. Just like God, the father reminds him, "You are always with me and whatever I have is yours." But like the sinner, the younger son was lost and is found again. This is cause for a celebration.

Mary Berendes has authored dozens of books for children, including nature titles as well as books about countries and holidays. She loves to collect antique books and has some that are almost 200 years old. Mary lives in Minnesota.

Robert Squier has been drawing ever since he could hold a crayon. Today, instead of using crayons, he uses pencils, paint, and the computer. Robert lives in New Hampshire with his wife.